Colour the Catwalk

Really Cool Colouring **Book 4**

First published in 2015 by Kyle Craig Publishing

Text and illustration copyright © 2015 Kyle Craig Publishing

Editor: Alison McNicol

Design: Julie Anson

ISBN: 978-1-908-707-91-8

A CIP record for this book is available from the British Library.

A Kyle Craig Publication

www.kyle-craig.com

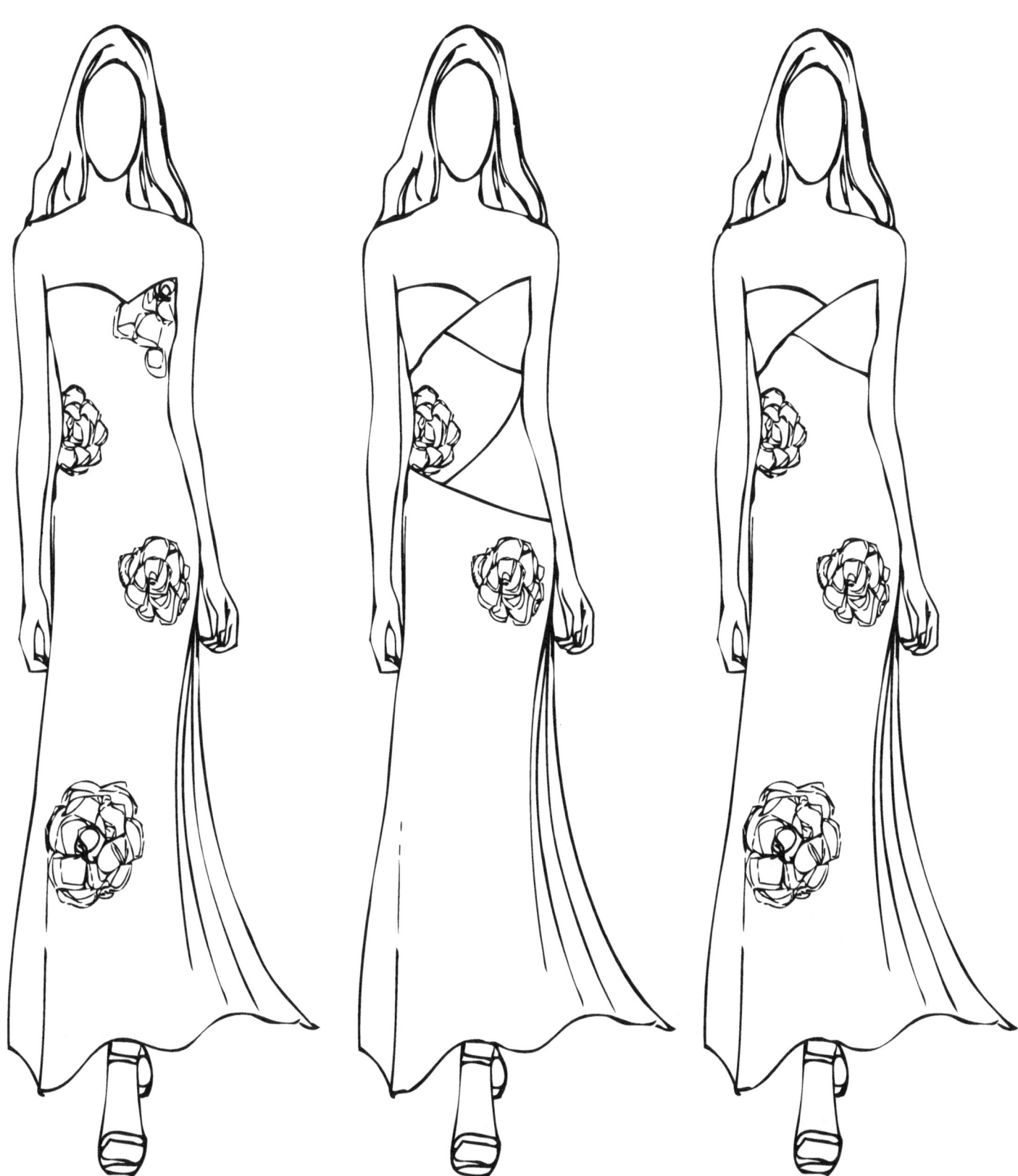

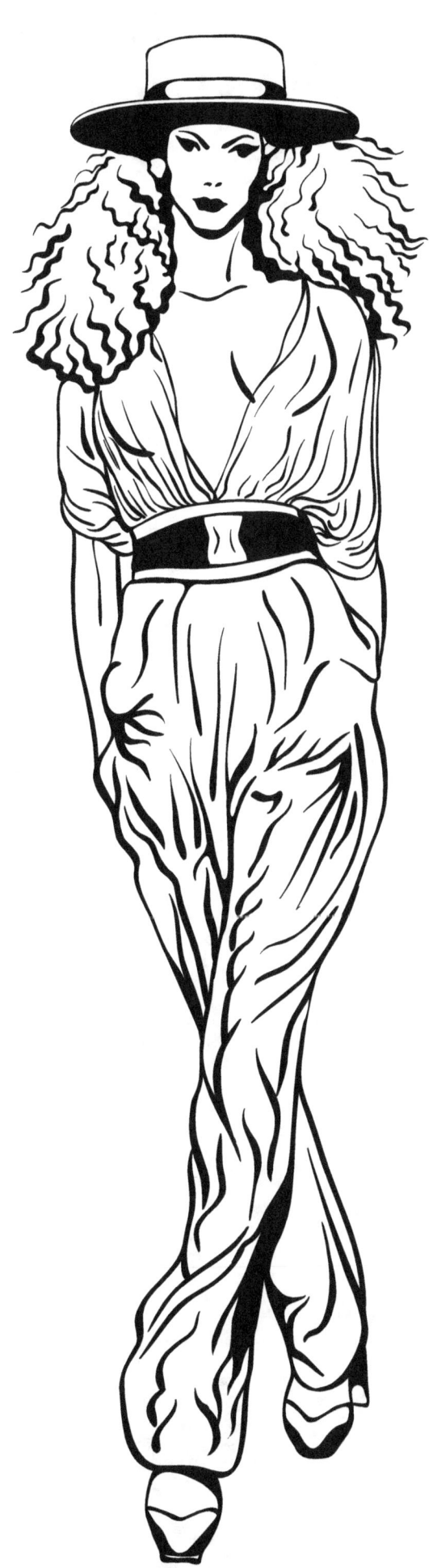

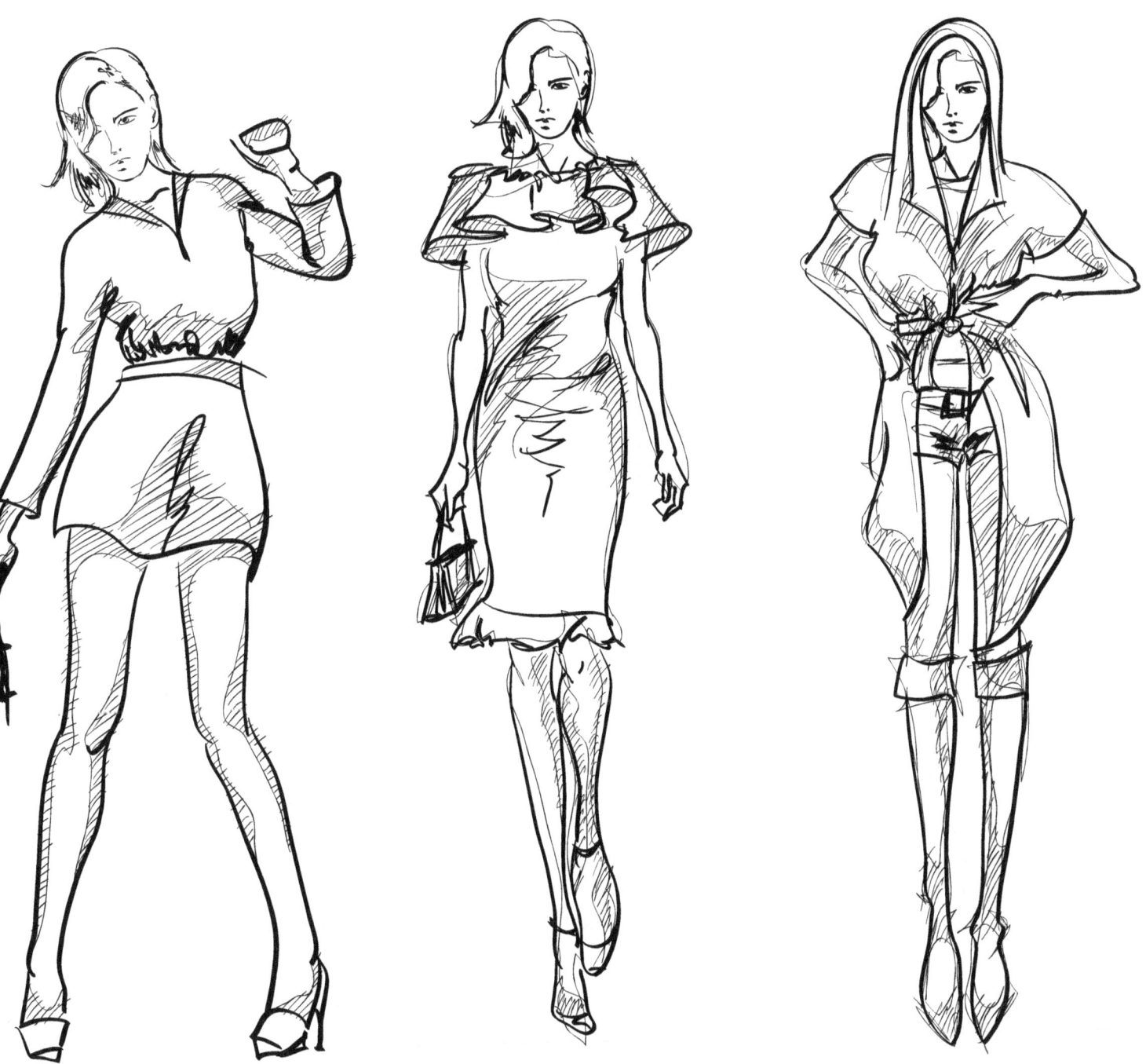